on the track of the mystery animal

by MIRIAM SCHLEIN

on the track of the mystery animal

THE STORY
OF THE DISCOVERY OF THE OKAPI

illustrated by RUTH SANDERSON

Four Winds Press   New York

LIBRARY OF CONGRESS CATALOGING IN PUBLICATION DATA

Schlein, Miriam.
  On the track of the mystery animal.

  Bibliography: p.
  Includes index.
  SUMMARY: Describes Sir Harry Johnston's efforts to locate
and identify the okapi, a member of the giraffe family found
deep in Central Africa's rain forest.
  1. Okapi—Juvenile literature. 2. Johnston, Harry Hamilton,
Sir, 1858-1927—Juvenile literature. 3. Zoologists—Great Bri-
tain—Biography—Juvenile literature. [1. Okapi. 2. Johnston,
Harry Hamilton, Sir, 1858-1927] I. Sanderson, Ruth.
II. Title.
QL737.U56S35   599'.7357   78-5387
              ISBN 0-590-07488-1

PUBLISHED BY FOUR WINDS PRESS
A DIVISION OF SCHOLASTIC MAGAZINES, INC., NEW YORK, N.Y.
TEXT COPYRIGHT © 1978 BY MIRIAM SCHLEIN
ILLUSTRATIONS COPYRIGHT © 1978 BY RUTH SANDERSON
ALL RIGHTS RESERVED
PRINTED IN THE UNITED STATES OF AMERICA
LIBRARY OF CONGRESS CATALOG CARD NUMBER: 78-5387
1   2   3   4   5   82   81   80   79   78

Contents

Only the Pygmies Knew

Can you find the mystery animal?

It has stripes on its backside and legs. Is it some kind of zebra?

It has very big ears. Is it some kind of donkey or ass?

It is more or less the size of a horse. Is it some kind of big-eared, striped horse?

It is none of these things.

It is an okapi.

The okapi was one of the last animals to be discovered by modern man. In fact, for a long time, it was a sort of "mystery animal." No one really knew what it was.

Why was that?

There is only one place in the world where the okapi lives: deep in the tropical rain forest in central Africa. To anyone not accustomed to the rain forest, it is a mysterious and dangerous place. Not many people from the outside world ever go into it.

In many spots the ground growth is so thick, you must hack your way through. The trees are gigantic. Their uppermost leaves meet 100 feet up, blocking out the sunlight. And so except in clearings, the rain forest is rather dark. Thick vines grow up and about. You cannot see for any long distance because the thick green forest grows like a wall all about you.

Once in a while, some explorers did make their way into the rain forest. When they came out, they would tell of unusual creatures they had seen—leopards, bongos, dwarf buffalo, snakes and all kinds of bright-colored birds. Sometimes they saw an animal that looked something like a horse. They did not know what this animal was. And it was so shy, and ran away so quickly, they could never get a good look at it. One explorer might get just a glimpse of some stripes, and he would say he saw some kind of zebra. Another explorer might get a quick look and remember that the animal had very large ears, and so he thought it might be a kind of wild donkey—or ass. But none of them could ever get near enough to see it at close range. And so this animal remained one of the mysteries of the rain forest.

We should not say that no one knew anything about this animal. There are people who live right in the rain forest. These are the small people called pygmies. They know the rain forest, and to them it is not a frightening place. They move about it with ease. And they live by hunting, fishing, and gathering mushrooms, berries and other forest foods.

The pygmies had known about this animal for thousands of years. To them it was no mystery. They trapped it in shallow

pits, and ate the meat, and used the skin. They had a name for this animal. It sounded like "okwapi." But the pygmies had very little contact with people from outside the rain forest. And so it was here, in this one special place, hidden from most people, that the okapi had lived for thousands of years, known to no one but the pygmies.

Is It a Unicorn?

In 1901, there were headlines in the London newspapers:

NEW MAMMAL DISCOVERED!

People were excited and wanted to know more: What was the new animal? Who discovered it? What was it like?

The animal was discovered by an Englishman named Sir Harry Johnston.

How does someone "discover" an animal?

The story of how Sir Harry Johnston discovered the okapi is like a detective story. Like other detectives, he had some false clues, and he followed some false trails. But he kept working at his problem. And, as in other detective stories, he finally solved the mystery when he had some good, solid evidence.

Harry Johnston was born in London in 1858. As a boy, he was interested in animals and read a lot of books about them. One book in particular interested him. It told about the strange animals that were just being discovered in different parts of the world. One explorer, for example, had just discovered the great gorillas in western Africa. According to the book's author, Philip Gosse, there were probably even more new animals — that is, animals still unknown to modern man — hidden deep in the jungle. He noted that Dutch, Portuguese, and French traders had been coming back to Europe with stories about an unusual animal they had seen in the African rain forest. It was a horse, they said, with horns. Philip Gosse advanced the theory that this animal might be a unicorn.

"The Unicorn in Captivity," from THE HUNT OF THE UNICORN *tapestries.*

Harry Johnston knew of the unicorn as a storybook animal, an animal appearing in old Greek myths. In these stories, it had a white, horselike body, the tail of a lion, blue eyes, and a single 30-inch-long spiraled horn growing out from its forehead. This horn was believed to have magical powers: dip it in water, and it would make the water pure. Dip it in any liquid, and it would show if poison were there.

Harry wondered. Could there be a real, living unicorn? And if this rain forest animal was not a unicorn, then what was it?

This question lingered in Harry's mind long after he finished the book.

When Harry was eleven, he had a bad case of scarlet fever. When he was better, the doctor advised that he stay out of school for a year so that he could get back his strength. During this year, Harry's aunt, who was studying to be an artist, sometimes took Harry with her to art school. He began to learn to draw and found that he liked it. Since he was interested in animals he started spending days at the zoo, making drawings of the animals.

One afternoon as Harry was sitting at his easel drawing the head of a lion, one of the professors connected with the zoo stopped to admire his work. The professor invited Harry to come to a special lab where, along with other students, he could learn more about the structure of animals and birds. Harry did this. Soon be began to get commissions from some of the scientists at the Zoological Society to make drawings to illustrate books and articles they were writing.

One commission was to make drawings of chimpanzee brains. Another assignment was for a doctor who was doing a study of unusual hair growth. There are, it seems, many people whose entire bodies, except for the face and front of the neck, are completely covered with thick hair, like an ape. Harry's job was to make drawings showing the exact direction of the hair growth.

In 1875, Harry entered King's College, where he studied French, Italian, Spanish, and Portuguese in the evenings. During the days, he continued his work at the zoo. He also kept on studying painting at the Royal Academy in London.

When he was 18, he spent a few months in Spain. He found that he loved to travel. In 1879, he went to Tunisia in North Africa, where he painted and also studied architecture and language. He wrote articles about things he saw and sold them to an English newspaper, *The Globe.* He also sold some of his paintings.

Three years later, he joined an expedition to Angola. In 1883, when he was 25, on a different expedition, Harry spent some time with Henry Stanley, who was then exploring the Congo River.

In those times, before photography was as good as it is now, it was customary for an artist to accompany expeditions to record in drawings the wildlife, the geographical features, and the people of different places. Harry Johnston, with his good powers of observation, his keen interest in animals, and his artistic ability, was a valued member on these expeditions. His knowledge of languages was also helpful, and on these expeditions he began his study of the Bantu languages used in Africa — something he kept working on his entire life. The following year Johnston himself led a scientific expedition to Mount Kilimanjaro. While there, he had formal discussions with native chiefs and arranged trading treaties with them.

This was the time in history when the British Empire spread out to many distant parts of the world.* And it was not uncommon for many Englishmen to travel and explore and to rule in many strange and far-off places.

*Other countries — France, Germany, Portugal, Belgium, and the Netherlands — were also establishing colonies in Africa at this time.

In 1885, when Harry Johnston was 27 years old, he was appointed British vice-consul in Cameroon.

In 1888, a book by Henry Stanley the explorer was published. It was called *In Darkest Africa*. In it, Stanley tells about his explorations, his discoveries, and his adventures in Africa. It is a long book, and at the end of it, there are some brief notes. One of them says this:

The Wambutti* know a donkey and call it "Atti." They say they sometimes catch them in pits.

Harry Johnston read this and wondered: Could this "donkey" be that same mystery animal that the old Portuguese and Dutch explorers told about: the horned horse that lived in the rain forest—their "unicorn"?

There was something else that puzzled him. A donkey is a domesticated ass. An ass is part of the horse family. And this sort of animal typically lives in herds out on open plains where it can run. Why then did this particular ass or donkey live deep in the rain forest? Something seemed wrong. It was not a normal place for this type of animal to live.

This is what Harry Johnston wrote, in a magazine article:

... the occurrence of anything like a horse or ass—animals so partial to treeless, grassy plains—in the depths of the mightiest forest of the world seemed to me so strange that I determined to make further inquiries on the subject whenever fate should lead me in the direction of the great Kongo forest.

It happened that fate did lead Harry Johnston in the direction of the Congo forest. But fate did even better than that. It led him right to the pygmies—the only people in the world who really knew anything about this mystery animal.

*A pygmy tribe. Sometimes called Bambuti.

The Kidnapped Pygmies

In 1899, Harry Johnston was appointed special commissioner of the Uganda Protectorate. He was now 41 years old. He was also now to be called *Sir* Harry Johnston, for in 1896 he had been made a knight for his service to Britain.

His new post, Uganda, lay just to the east of the Congo. As soon as he got to his headquarters in Entebbe, the following thing happened. A German went into the Congo and kidnapped some pygmies. He wanted to take them back to Europe and exhibit them at the Paris Exhibition. The Congo* was then under the rule of Belgium, and so the Belgian government sent local troops to stop the German from doing this. But before they could catch him, he managed to get over the border to Uganda, where he thought he would be safe. The Belgians contacted Sir Harry Johnston and asked his official help in rescuing the pygmies.

Sir Harry immediately sent word to commanders of various posts throughout Uganda. The German kidnapper was found, taken into custody, and brought back with the pygmies to Johnston's headquarters in Entebbe. The German was tried in court and made to pay a large fine. The pygmies were released into Sir Harry Johnston's care.

Sir Harry had promised the Belgian government that he would see to it that the pygmies got safely back to their home and their people in the rain forest. In fact, he promised that he would escort them back in person. But because of official duties,

*It is now an independent nation called Zaire.

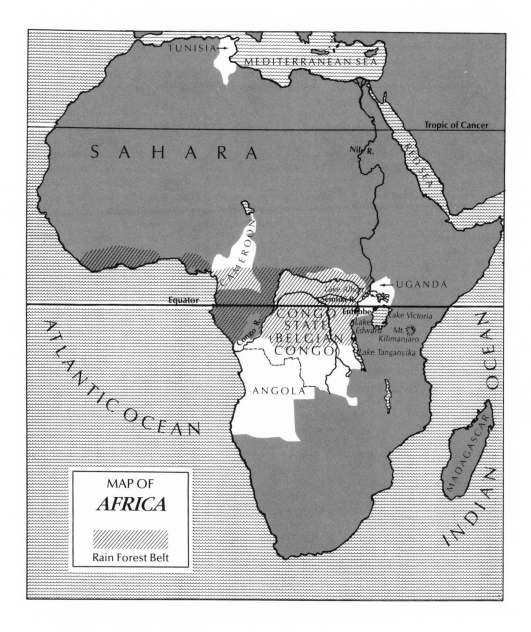

MAP OF
AFRICA

Rain Forest Belt

he could not leave immediately. So for the time being, the pygmies settled down in a roughly cleared "park" behind Sir Harry Johnston's house. It was like a little zoo, with an elephant, a zebra, and a baby hippo roaming around in it. There were also pythons and some other snakes — but these were kept in cages.

While the pygmies were with him, Sir Harry wanted to learn all he could about the mystery animal. Although Johnston had made a study of the Bantu languages, the pygmies spoke a form of Bantu language not known to Johnston. So at first they could communicate with each other only in sign language. Johnston did speak Swahili — the language used by government officials and traders in that area. It is a language made up partly of Arabic and partly of Bantu languages. And the pygmies were very quick in learning to speak to Johnston in Swahili.

13

When he asked them about the donkeylike animal, the "Atti," they knew which animal he meant. They told him that their name for it in their language was "o'api."* They said it was striped like a zebra, except for the upper parts of the body, which were a solid, dark, purplish brown. But what interested Harry Johnston most was the way they described the animal's feet. They said it had "more than one hoof."

*pronounced "okwapi," or "okapi."

14

He knew what they meant by that: they meant that the animal did not have a single, undivided hoof like the horse does.

"More than one hoof." He thought about that. Perhaps its feet had two toes—a divided hoof like the giraffe, or the antelope. Perhaps it had three hoofed toes, like the rhino. But if this were a fact, if the okapi did have "more than one hoof," that automatically meant that it could not be a horse. Nor could it be any of the animals related to the present-day horse,

15

like the zebra, the ass, or donkey, because all these animals have a single undivided hoof.

What was it, then?

Harry Johnston knew that the earliest ancestor to the horse — a small creature we call *Eohippus* — lived about 50 million years ago. It was no bigger than a large dog, and it had a different kind of toe formation than the horse does now. Instead of the single, undivided hoof of the present-day horse, *Eohippus* had four toes on the front feet and three toes on its hind feet.

The hoof is the horny covering of an animal's toes.

As millions of years passed, the horse gradually changed.* It became larger, and its toe formation changed. After a while, it had three toes on each foot, with the middle toe becoming longer and stronger than the other toes. The horse's full weight now rested on this one strong hoofed middle toe. Having this strong middle toe and undivided hoof covering helped the horse to survive, for, with it, the horse could run fast over long distances to escape enemies.

Up until one or two million years ago, there was still a kind of horse — the *Hipparion* — that had three toes.

---

*These changes that take place in an animal over millions of years' time come about by means of a process we call "evolution."

The tiny EOHIPPUS *had four-toed and three-toed feet.*

Thinking of all this, Sir Harry got a strange and exciting idea: Could the mystery animal possibly be a living survivor of the *Hipparion* — the three-toed horse of long ago? The horse everyone thought was extinct? What a discovery that would be!

Now he was all the more eager to get to the Congo. But he still could not leave Entebbe. During these few months when the pygmies were waiting for him, one of them died. He had been sick when he arrived. He had gotten internal injuries while he was with the German. It was a sad event. Sir Harry asked the remaining pygmies how they would feel if he sent the skeleton of their dead brother far off to England, to a big house where all different types of mankind were studied.

The pygmies had a council among themselves. Then they told Sir Harry that it would be an honor to their dead brother. Today, the skeleton of that pygmy is still in the Natural History Museum in London.

Tracking Through the Forest

In July, Sir Harry was finally able to take the pygmies back to their home in the rain forest. They traveled into the Congo, up the right bank of the Semliki River. Then they crossed by canoe to a Belgian station camp on the edge of the rain forest. The man in charge here was Lieutenant Meura. His second-in-command was Lieutenant Karl Eriksson. Having someone new to talk to was a treat for them stationed as they were in the wilderness. When Harry Johnston asked them about the mystery animal, they were vague. Even they, living where they did, right at the forest's edge, had never seen a living okapi. But they had seen dead ones. The native soldiers sometimes shot these animals and brought them back into camp. Because of its stripes, Meura and Eriksson had always assumed it was some kind of zebra. In fact, they added, the soldiers had killed one just recently.

Of course Johnston was eager to see it. But he was a little too late. The soldiers had already cut up the animal and eaten the meat. They used the skin to make themselves a type of military shoulder belts called bandoliers.

Sir Harry was disappointed not to see the animal. Still, he was excited to hold in his hand at least a part of its skin. He felt he was coming closer to the mystery animal. He bought two of the bandoliers from the soldiers.

Then Lieutenant Meura had a suggestion. "Why don't you track down the animal yourself? Some of the native soldiers here will go with you and guide you. You will also be taking the pygmies closer to their home territory."

Johnston thought this was an excellent idea. He went into the rain forest, guided by the pygmies and the men from Meura's camp. This is what he wrote about the trip, later on:

The atmosphere of the forest was almost unbreathable with its Turkish-bath heat, its reeking moisture, and its powerful smell of decaying, rotting vegetation. We seemed, in fact, to be transported back to Miocene* times, to an age and a climate scarcely suitable for the modern type of real humanity.

For several days they searched through the rain forest. Although they did not see the mystery animal itself, the pygmies and Meura's men showed Johnston some tracks.

"These are the tracks of the animal," they said. "These are the tracks we should follow."

Johnston bent down to look closely. It was a tense moment. If it was the track of a present-day horse or zebra or ass, it would be a single, undivided hoofprint. If it was the track of the prehistoric *Hipparion,* it would be a three-toed hoofprint.

He did not know which one he expected to see.

It was neither.

Instead, he saw what looked like the ordinary track that could have been made by any of the two-toed, cloven (divided) — hoofed animals.

Johnston was both disappointed and angry.

"You're trying to fool me," he said, as he stood up. "This is just the trail of some ordinary forest antelope."

"No, no," they insisted. "This was made by an okapi."

---

*Miocene: the time in the Earth's past between 26 million and 5 million years ago.

It happened that the guides and the pygmies were 100 percent right. It was, in fact, the track of an okapi. But they could not convince Johnston of this. He refused to follow the trail.

What to do now? From here the pygmies could go on alone to their own part of the forest. They said good-bye to Johnston and set out for their home. But before anything else could be decided by Johnston and the rest of his party, the group got terribly sick with malaria and could not go on. They could not even get back to camp by themselves. A messenger managed to go back for help. Soldiers and station workers were sent from camp to carry Johnston and the others out of the rain forest.

They remained too sick to get to Uganda by themselves and had to be helped back to Entebbe by Belgian troops. It was a disappointing ending to the trip.

Johnston had achieved one thing: He had helped the pygmies get back to their home. But he had not accomplished the other thing that was so important to him. Aside from acquiring two strips of skin cut into bandoliers, he had not really found out anything much about the mystery animal.

Lieutenant Meura saw how disappointed Johnston was. And he promised, as they were saying good-bye, that he would make every effort to get hold of a perfect okapi skin soon, and send it to Johnston at Entebbe.

A New Kind of Horse?

Meanwhile, Johnston did have the bandoliers. When he got back to Entebbe, he sent them to London in the diplomatic pouch with the mail. He wanted to show the scientists there that he was really on the track of a new animal.

In those days, the diplomatic pouch would go by messenger slowly overland through Africa, till it got to the coast. Then it went on a slow boat to London. Months later, in 1900, the two bandoliers arrived on the desk of Dr. Philip L. Sclater of the Zoological Society of London.

What would Dr. Sclater do with them?

In order to have a better understanding of living things, and to be able to study them in a more organized way, scientists in the 1700s and 1800s had started to "classify" plants and animals. This means examining them to decide which ones are closely related to one another, and then listing them in various groups, or "classifications."

Animals were considered to be closely related if they had certain things in common—certain kinds of horns, for example, or a certain kind of tooth arrangement, or a certain type of hoof. The more things the animals had in common, the more closely related they were considered to be.

One large group is the **class** of mammals.

Mammals are all animals that have the following things in common:

1. They have lungs and must breathe air.

2. They give birth to young like themselves (instead of laying eggs, as fish or turtles do); and they feed these young with milk from the mother's body.

3. They are all warm-blooded. (This means their body temperature stays fairly constant, and does not change with the warmth or coldness of the environment.)

Dogs are mammals, whales are mammals; elephants and mice and giraffes are mammals. People are mammals. There are between four and five thousand different kinds of mammals.

All these mammals are then divided into separate groups called **orders**. There are about 19 different orders. All the mammals in one order are alike in certain additional ways.

Here are the two orders that concerned Sclater and Johnston, for they knew that the mystery animal had hoofs:

The order of Perissodactyla: These are all the hoofed mammals that have an odd number of toes on each foot. Horses, zebras, asses, rhinos, and tapirs are in this order.

The order of Artiodactyla: These are all the hoofed mammals that have an even number of toes on each foot. Hippos, giraffes, deer, pigs, and camels are some of the animals in this order.

Animals in certain orders are then divided into groups called **families.** Animals within one family have even more things in common.

Let's look at the family groups in the two orders of hoofed animals as they were known to Johnston and Sclater:

Order of Perissodactyla:

a. Family of Equidae (horselike animals)

b. Family of Tapiridae (tapirs and others)

c. Family of Rhinocerotidae (rhinos and others)

Order of Artiodactyla:

a. Family of Suidae
(pigs and others)

b. Family of Hippopotamidae
(hippos and others)

c. Family of Cervidae
(deer and others)

d. Family of Giraffidae (giraffes)

e. Family of Bovidae (antelope, cows, goats, and others)

And more. There are 9 Recent families in this order.

Animals in each family are then divided up into more separate groups called **genera**. (*Genus* is the singular for this word.) Animals in the same genus are alike in even more ways.

In the Equidae family there is only one Recent genus. This genus is named *Equus*.

In the Cervidae family, however, there are 17 different genera. The caribou, the moose, and the white-tailed deer, for example, are in different genera of the family Cervidae.

Some families are large and have many genera; some families are small with few.

Animals in each genus are then divided into more separate groups called **species**. Animals within one species are so closely related that they are able to breed with one another and reproduce young.

In the genus *Equus*, there are eight different Recent species. These include various species of horses, zebras, and asses.

Now we go back to Dr. Sclater in London in 1900. On his table before him, he has two strips of skin and fur which had been made into bandoliers. From this, he was expected to come up with some idea of what type of animal they came from.

Sclater examined the bandoliers. Usually, two very important things to examine when trying to classify and identify an animal are the hoofs and the teeth. If Dr. Sclater had just had a hoof to look at, that would have been a big help. A hoof would immediately tell him which order the animal was in. If the hoof had three toes, he would know the animal should be classified in the order of Perissodactyla (hoofed mammals with an odd number of toes). If the hoof had two or four toes, he would know it should be classified in the order of Artiodactyla (hoofed mammals with an even number of toes).

But Sclater had no hoof. Not even one tooth. All he had were two strips of skin. It was not much to go on.

He examined the hair closely under a microscope. Although the skin had stripes, Sclater decided that this animal was not a zebra. The hair was not exactly the same as the hair of a zebra. But it was very similar. So Sclater felt it must belong to an animal which was not a zebra, but similar to it.

Since the zebra is in the genus *Equus* in the horse family (Equidae), Sclater felt this new animal was also in the horse family, but not within any of the known species. So he gave it the name *Equus (?) johnstoni. Equus* as the genus name, to show it was a horselike animal, and *johnstoni* as the species name of this horselike animal—named after its discoverer.

More Clues

Do you think Sclater was a little hasty in deciding what John-ston's mystery animal was? After all, he only had two band-oliers — not much evidence to go on. In fact, Sclater did admit he was not really positive about this classification. He had doubts. Did you notice how he indicated his doubt? He called this animal *Equus (?) johnstoni.*

There was also another opinion to back up this classifica-tion. Henry Stanley, who had explored the Congo, also thought this animal was some kind of forest ass. If that were so, it would also put the animal in the genus *Equus.*

Just a few months after this, Harry Johnston got some valuable new evidence. He got a complete skin of an okapi. And he got two okapi skulls. They were sent to him by Lieuten-ant Karl Eriksson, who had been Lieutenant Meura's second-in-command at the Belgian outpost in the Congo. Within this short time, Meura himself had died of black-water fever. But Eriksson had remembered Meura's promise to Johnston. And when a native brought a dead okapi into camp, Eirksson had seen to it that the skin was carefully removed and the skull kept. These, along with teeth and hoofs, he sent to Harry John-ston.

Before packing these things, Eriksson looked them over. He was surprised when he saw that the hoofs were "cloven," or divided into two toes. This meant that the animal could not be a zebra as he and Meura had assumed. It could not be anything

30

This is what his drawing looked like.

in the horse family at all. For the two-toed hoof clearly put it in the order of Artiodactyla, the even-toed hoofed mammals. Eriksson enclosed a note to Johnston in which he mentioned this observation.

Unfortunately, Johnston was not at Entebbe when the package arrived. Someone else opened it. The hoofs dried up, dropped off the body, and were lost.

Still, there was a lot to work with.

When Johnston returned, he laid out the skin and the skull. From these remains of the dead animal, he tried to imagine what the living animal looked like. And he drew a picture of it.

Johnston was now in a much better position to identify the mystery animal than Sclater had been only a few months before. For he now had several vital things. Although he did not have the hoofs themselves, he had Eriksson's note. He knew it was a divided hoof, which automatically put the animal outside of the horse family.*

He also had teeth.

Teeth are important. You can learn a lot by examining teeth, because different animals have different kinds of teeth.

Johnston saw that this animal had bilobed, lower canine teeth. This is a feature found only in the giraffe.

There was even more evidence in these teeth. Some of them had a bumpy, almost wrinkled quality. Scientists call this "rugosity." This also is a feature found only in giraffe teeth.

Then, Harry Johnston picked up the skull. This was the best clue of all, because he could plainly see three "horn-cores" making up part of the skull. These are knobby, bony bumps, two on top and one between the eyes.

Johnston knew there was only one animal that had horn-cores. That is the giraffe.

Every single clue pointed to some kind of animal very closely related to the giraffe. But there existed, as far as Johnston knew, no Recent species of animal related to the giraffe. The giraffe was the only known living animal in the Giraffidae family.

As long ago as the Miocene, there were animals related to the giraffe. They did not look exactly like our present-day giraffe. Some of them had large, forked antlers, like a deer's. And they did not have the long neck of our present-day giraffe. Some of them had sort of cowlike bodies. But all of these giraffelike relatives had been extinct for millions of years. Scien-

*Remember, animals in the horse family are in the order of Perissodactyla—animals with an odd number of toes.

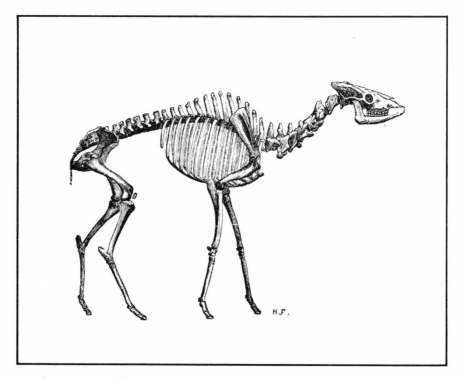

A reconstructed HELLADOTHERIUM *skeleton. Notice the line of the neck.*

tists in Johnston's time knew such animals had existed, because of fossils that were dug up in Greece, Spain, China, and what is now Israel. By examining these fossils, scientists could tell they were the bones of animals in the giraffe family.

Harry Johnston knew that fossil remains of an animal called the *Helladotherium* had just recently been found in Greece and also in India. The *Helladotherium* had been in the giraffe family. But it had a shorter neck than the present-day giraffe. It had lived before the Ice Age, when more of the earth was tropical, in the time we call the Miocene. The *Helladotherium* had been extinct for millions of years.

34

But was it?

The rain forest now—as Johnston himself had noted—was very much like what we imagine the world to have been like during the Miocene. Perhaps this Miocene animal had lived on, hidden in the rain forest, unknown to modern man.

Harry Johnston looked again and again at the skull and the skin stretched out before him. Could he dare to believe that they were the remains of a living, surviving *Helladotherium*—an animal thought to be extinct for millions and millions of years?

He sent the skulls and the skin to London for closer scientific examination. He also sent along the drawing he had made. This time he sent his finds to Professor Ray Lankester, director of the British Museum of Natural History. Johnston sent notes, too, outlining his own new theory. Since they now knew the animal was not in the horse family, the name *Equus* would have to be withdrawn.

He suggested a new name: *Helladotherium tigrenum* ("tigrenum" means "striped").

Lankester agreed with Johnston that this was no horse—no *Equus*. But he also knew it was not a surviving *Helladotherium*. The skull and the teeth were different from those of the *Helladotherium*. And although the animal that Johnston had sent to him—or rather, the remains of it—had many things in common with the giraffe, it was not a giraffe, either. It was a totally different animal.

It was, in fact, a new species of animal, one that science had not known about before. Its closest relative was the great, long-necked giraffe.

Who would have thought that?

Using the original pygmy word, Professor Lankester gave the animal its new scientific name: *Okapia johnstoni*.

It is classified in the family of animals called Giraffidae. The animals in this family have this in common: they have

35

5.5 meters
(18 feet)

3.7 meters
(12 feet)

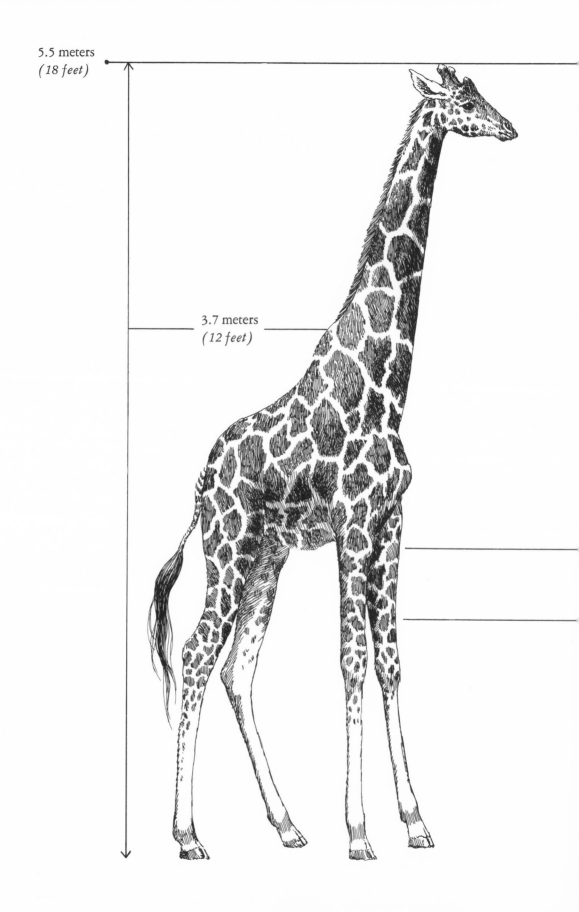

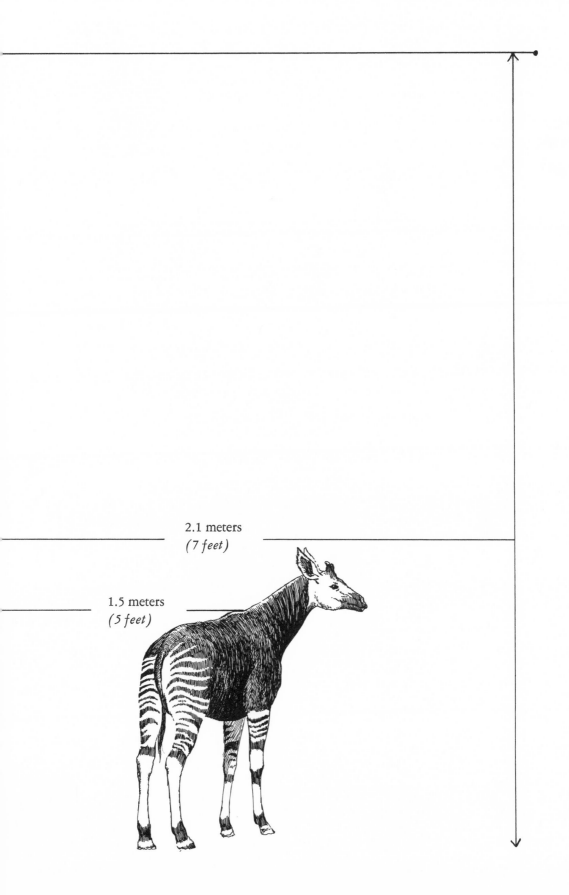

2.1 meters
(7 feet)

1.5 meters
(5 feet)

skin-covered, knoblike horns that are part of their skull and they have tooth rugosity.

In other ways, the two animals are quite different. The okapi does not have the giraffe's long neck. And it lives deep in the rain forest, rather than out in the open savannah, as the giraffe does.

There is only one living genus of giraffe, and one species within that genus.* Its scientific name is *Giraffa camelopardalis.* There is also only one living genus of okapi, and one species within that genus: *Okapia johnstoni.*

Giraffidae is a small family.

At the museum in London, the skin and the skull were mounted by Rowland Ward, who was a skilled taxidermist. He had no skeleton to work from. A number of scientists disagreed as to the general shape of the animal. Some thought the neck should be more or less upright, as it appeared in Johnston's drawing. But Rowland Ward felt positive that the neck line should slope along the same angle as the rest of the body—making a more or less continuous line with the back of the animal. That is the way he mounted it.

Johnston then did a second drawing of the okapi, this one with a sloping neck, based on Ward's reconstruction.

At the time, Johnston wrote this: "Until the okapi has been photographed alive or dead, it is difficult to say which of my two drawings is the more correct."**

The mystery animal was still a bit of a mystery.

---

*There are a few "sub-species" or "races" of giraffe that are different from one another in very slight ways. A different looking "design" on their coats, for example. But they are all in the same species. They are alike enough to mate with each other and bear young like themselves. This puts them in the same species.

**Several years later, when they saw a complete okapi, they knew the sloping-necked version was the more accurate one.

Johnston's second drawing of the okapi.

The Animal Who Lives Alone

What kind of animal is this okapi, that managed to avoid most of mankind for so long?

The okapi is a solitary animal. Look at this one. He spends most of his life wandering alone over okapi paths that twist and turn through the rain forest. Because of his coloration and markings, it is hard to see him against the thick vegetation. Now and then he will stop to quickly eat some sweet shoots, or fruits or seeds. Then he moves on.

In some places within the rain forest, the vegetation is not so thick. There are low, clear valleys, where streams run through. On the sides of the stream, lush grasses grow.

The okapi likes these places. He grazes on the grasses. And sometimes he follows the stream, walking in the water.

Now we can see him better. Striped buttocks, purplish body, the big ears and gentle eyes. When he takes his foot out of the water, we can see his divided hoof, with a black band around each foot, like four little black socks. Above that, the legs are white up to the knee; then the stripes begin. Every okapi has this same distinctive pattern.

Now he stops to wash himself. He doesn't do this in the stream. He washes himself with his tongue. Look at that tongue. It is long and pointy. It is also prehensile. That means he can grab things with it.* Because his tongue is so long, the okapi can reach up and wash his eyes with it. In fact, he can reach every part of his body with it. This is how he keeps his coat so sleek and clean—by tongue-washing. An okapi's tongue is sometimes 35 centimeters long—about 14 inches.

*His relative, the giraffe, has a long tongue like this, too.

We chew our food before we swallow it. The okapi does not. He pulls leaves into his mouth and swallows them immediately, without chewing. He has a stomach with four parts to it. The leaves he swallows go right down to his first stomach, called the "paunch," or sometimes to the second stomach.

When he is finished eating, he goes off to a safer, even more secluded place where he can relax. Then, he makes a sort of hiccup. The food, which has gotten softer while in his paunch, comes back up through his gullet, back into his mouth. It is in the form of a big soft ball. This is called a "bolus."

Now he takes his time in chewing it. He sort of grinds it, swinging his lower jaw to one side, then to the other. The food mixes with his saliva and gets even softer. Then he swallows it again. This time the food takes a shortcut. It goes along a groove on the roof of the second stomach, directly into the third and fourth stomachs. Here, the food finally gets digested.

Animals that have four-part stomachs and eat this way are called "ruminants." Giraffe, deer, cows, and a number of other animals are ruminants. People sometimes say a cow is "chewing her cud." What she is really doing is chewing the bolus that she has hiccuped back up into her mouth from her paunch.

The okapi does not sleep for long periods of time, the way we do. He takes short little naps, sometimes for just a few minutes, probably standing up. Even while he is sleeping, his senses of smell and hearing do not relax totally. That is why it is so hard to sneak up to capture him.

No matter what he is doing, or where he is, the okapi must always stay alert, because he has enemies, lying in wait. He knows his enemies. They are snakes, and leopards, and sometimes man. It is mostly his ears and his nose that warn him of danger, rather than his eyes—for in the rain forest,

things are hidden. He has keen hearing and a good sense of smell. At any slight sign of danger—an odor or a rustling in the vegetation—he will run, dashing deeper into the rain forest along the okapi path. If it is too late to run, he will stand his ground and defend himself. He can attack with stabs of his horns. Or he can kick. He has powerful legs and hoofs.

The female okapi grows to be larger than the male. She is taller and heavier. But she has no horns. If she is attacked, she defends herself and her young by kicking.

The female okapi also wanders alone, except for the time when she has her calf or young one with her.

There is only one time of the year when okapis are not alone. This is around June, July, and August. It is the mating season. And they are all looking for mates.

How do they find each other as they wander alone through the tangled forest?

As the female walks through the forest, she leaves a trail of a strong scent that comes from glands in her feet. The male will not see her at first. But he will follow this smelling-trail*.

*Some animal experts think that during the mating season the female may also make loud bellowing or coughing noises, which the male will hear, and follow. This is not certain.

Finally, he catches up to her. They circle around one another. He licks her face. They get to know each other, by sight, by smell, by licking. Then they mate.

Sometimes, the male and the female will stay with each other for a while, wandering together. They might also have a yearling with them—a young okapi that had been born to the female the year before.

Sometimes, though, they just separate.

About fifteen months later, the new baby is born.

Okapis have only one baby at a time. The babies are usually born between August and October. This is the rainy season.

About 2 meters (around 80 inches) of rain falls in the rain forest during this time.

When it is time for the mother okapi to give birth, she goes into the thickest part of the forest. As soon as the baby is born, the first thing the mother okapi does is to clean it off. She licks off the blood and mucous so that enemies cannot smell it. Then she hides the baby in a safe place in the underbrush, and leaves it for a little while. She needs to eat.

She does not go very far. While mother and baby okapi are separated, they call out to each other, to keep in touch. The newborn baby okapi can make a coughing sound and a bleat like a lamb. Sometimes it makes a whistling kind of call. The mother answers back. She does not stay away too long.

Okapis do not wander around much in the rainy season the way they do the rest of the year. For when the rain is falling, it interferes with their sense of smell and their hearing, which normally protect them. And so at this time, they stay sheltered in the deepest part of the forest. Here, they feel safer.

Other rain forest animals do not move around much either, in the time of the heavy rains.

Baby okapi is a sturdy little creature. And not so little, really. This one is 76 centimeters (about 30 inches) tall at the shoulder. She weighs 16 kilograms (about 35 pounds).* She already has the markings of the adult okapi—striped buttocks, white legs. Aside from her size, she is different from the adult in only a few ways. Her neck is not as long and stretched out as her mother's. Her hair is longer than her mother's. And she has a mane down her neck to her back. She loses this later on. The adult okapi has no mane.

*The mother okapi is 160 centimeters (around 62 inches) tall at the shoulder, and weighs 225 kilograms (about 500 pounds).

In a few hours, she has her first meal of milk from her mother. In about six weeks, she will also be eating some leafy forest food. In four months, she will be able to ruminate, like an adult. And when she is ready, she will leave her mother to follow her own solitary life along the okapi trails of the rain forest.

Although more than 75 years have gone by since the okapi was discovered, there are still some important things we do not know about them. This is because it is so difficult for anyone to get close to them for a long enough time to be able to observe the patterns and rhythms of their life in the wild, as scientists are able to do with many other kinds of animals. One thing we do not know, for example, is how long a baby okapi stays with its mother before it is ready to go out on its own.

To the okapi, the rain forest is a haven. A protected place. It is a unique environment to which this animal is uniquely suited. And so, even now, hidden deep in the rain forest, the okapi has been able in some ways, to remain a mystery animal.

Where can you see an okapi?

Some zoos in the United States that had okapis at the time this book was being written are the Brookfield Zoo in Chicago, the Colorado Springs Zoo, the Dallas Zoo, the San Diego Zoo, the Oklahoma City Zoo, and Bush Gardens in Tampa, Florida.

The zoos in the following European cities also had okapis: Antwerp, Belgium; Basle, Switzerland; Berlin, East Germany; Bristol, England; Paris, France; Rotterdam, Netherlands; Duisburg, Germany; Frankfurt, Germany; Madrid, Spain.

CLASSIFICATION CHART

CLASS

MAMMALIA   There are between 4,000 and 5,000 species of mammals.   This number is not exact because scientists do not all agree on some of these groupings. Some scientists separate animals into a larger number of species because of small differences.

ORDER

There are 19 different orders in the class of mammals.

| *Perrissodactyla* The odd-toed, hoofed mammals: horses, zebras, asses, rhinos, and others. | *Cetacea* Whales, porpoises, and dolphins. | *Artiodactyla* The even-toed hoofed mammals: camels, deer, goats, pigs, hippos, okapis, giraffes, and others. | *Primates* Monkeys, man, gorillas, and others. | *Proboscidea* Elephants. | And others |

FAMILY

There are 9 different families in the order of Artiodactyla.

| *Bovidae:* Sheep, goats, antelope, cattle, and others. | *Camelidae:* Camels, alpacas, and others. | *Giraffidae:* Giraffes and okapis. | *Suidae:* Pigs, hogs, boars, and others. | *Cervidae:* Deer, reindeer, elks, moose, and others. | *Hippopotamidae:* Hippos and pygmy hippos. | And others |

GENUS

There are 82 different genera in the order of Artiodactyla. Only two of these are in Giraffidae family.

| *Giraffa* | *Okapia* |

SPECIES

There is only one species in the genus of Okapia.

Okapia johnstoni

*Note: There are classifications or groupings even larger than Class. The three basic groupings are *Kingdoms: animal, plant,* or *mineral.* The okapi is in the *animal kingdom.*

Each kingdom is then divided into further grouping or divisions called *phyla.* (The singular for this is *phylum.*) All creatures that have a backbone at some stage of their development are in the phylum *Chordata.* Okapi is in this phylum.

If that backbone is made up of separate units called *vertebrae,* the creature is in the subphylum *Vertebrata.* Okapi is in this subphylum.

This subphylum is further divided into classes. Okapi is in the class of Mammalia (mammals).

Bibliography

Bruens, A. "Curious Farm Run by Lay Brother in Belgian Congo." *Catholic World,* October 1941.

Burton, Maurice and Burton, Robert, eds. *International Wildlife Encyclopedia.* New York: Marshall Cavendish Corp., 1969.

Gatti, A. "Congo Okapi." *Nature, July* 1937.

_____. "Strangest Animal in Africa." *Travel,* April 1937.

Grzimek, Dr. H. C. Bernhard, ed. *Grzimek's Animal Life Encyclopedia.* Vol. 13. New York: Van Nostrand Reinhold, 1972.

Johnston, Sir Harry H. "The Okapi: The Newly Discovered Beast Living in Central Africa." *Smithsonian Annual Report,* 1901. Reprinted from *McClure's Magazine,* September 1901.

_____. *The Story of My Life.* Indianapolis: Bobbs-Merrill Company, 1923.

"A New Mammal." *London Times,* 7 May 1901.

Spinage, C. A. *The Book of the Giraffe.* Boston: Houghton Mifflin Company, 1968.

Walker, Ernest P., ed. *Mammals of the World.* 3d ed. Baltimore and London: The Johns Hopkins University Press, 1975.

Index